GREAT AMERICANS

HOW TO USE YOUR SD-X READER WITH THIS BOOK

This highly interactive book lets you explore American biographies in an interactive format. You can read the book and study the photographs and illustrations, but a touch of the SD-X Reader adds in-depth audio information, word definitions, and learning games to the page.

1. **Press the Power button to turn the SD-X Reader on or off. The LED will light up when the SD-X Reader is on.**

2. **Touch the volume buttons found on this page or on the Table of Contents page to adjust the volume.**

3. **Touch photographs and illustrations to hear additional information. Page headers and words or phrases that are in a different size or color than the surrounding text often provide a definition or more information.**

4. **As you explore the page, you'll encounter games and quizzes. Touch the text or image that started the game to stop playing.**

5. **After two minutes of inactivity, the Reader will beep and go to sleep.**

6. **If the batteries are low, the Reader will beep twice and the LED will start blinking. Replace the batteries by following the instructions on the next page. The SD-X Reader uses two AAA batteries.**

7. **To use headphones or earbuds, plug them into the headphone jack on the bottom of the SD-X Reader.**

CHANGE THE VOLUME WITH THESE BUTTONS

UP **DOWN**

Battery Information
Interactive Pen includes 2 replaceable AAA batteries (UM-4 or LR03).

Battery Installation
1. Open battery door with small flat-head or Phillips screwdriver.
2. Install new batteries according to +/- polarity. If batteries are not installed properly, the device will not function.
3. Replace battery door; secure with small screw.

Battery Safety
Batteries must be replaced by adults only. Properly dispose of used batteries. Do not dispose of batteries in fire; batteries may explode or leak. See battery manufacturer for disposal recommendations. Do not mix alkaline, standard (carbon-zinc), or rechargeable (nickel-cadmium) batteries. Do not mix old and new batteries. Only recommended batteries of the same or equivalent type should be used. Remove weakened or dead batteries. Never short-circuit the supply terminals. Non-rechargeable batteries are not to be recharged. Do not use rechargeable batteries. If batteries are swallowed, in the USA, promptly see a doctor and have the doctor phone 1-202-625-3333 collect. In other countries, have the doctor call your local poison control center. Batteries should be changed when sounds mix, distort, or become otherwise unintelligible as batteries weaken. The electrostatic discharge may interfere with the sound module. If this occurs, please simply restart the product.

In Europe, the dustbin symbol indicates that batteries, rechargeable batteries, button cells, battery packs, and similar materials must not be discarded in household waste. Batteries containing hazardous substances are harmful to the environment and to health. Please help to protect the environment from health risks by telling your children to dispose of batteries properly and by taking batteries to local collection points. Batteries handled in this manner are safely recycled.

Warning: Changes or modifications to this unit not expressly approved by the party responsible for compliance could void the user's authority to operate the equipment.

NOTE: This equipment has been tested and found to comply with the limits for a Class B digital device, pursuant to Part 15 of the FCC Rules. These limits are designed to provide reasonable protection against harmful interference in a residential installation. This equipment generates, uses, and can radiate radio frequency energy and, if not installed and used in accordance with the instructions, may cause harmful interference to radio communications. However, there is no guarantee that interference will not occur in a particular installation. If this equipment does cause harmful interference to radio or television reception, which can be determined by turning the equipment off and on, the user is encouraged to try to correct the interference by one or more of the following measures: Reorient or relocate the receiving antenna. Increase the separation between the equipment and receiver. Connect the equipment into an outlet on a circuit different from that to which the receiver is connected. Consult the dealer or an experienced radio TV technician for help.

Cover and interior art: Library of Congress; Shutterstock.com; Smithsonian Institution

Louis Weber, CEO
Publications International, Ltd.
8140 Lehigh Avenue
Morton Grove, IL 60053

Customer service: customer_service@pubint.com

ISBN: 978-1-68022-387-3

Manufactured in China.

8 7 6 5 4 3 2 1

CONTENTS

CHANGE THE VOLUME WITH THESE BUTTONS

UP

DOWN

INTRODUCTION

Great Americans tells the stories of hundreds of Americans whose accomplishments have helped shape the United States culturally, politically, and morally. Though just a fraction of many Americans who might be considered "great," they were included here because they excelled in their chosen field, acted as trailblazers, or influenced America's course in some significant way.

Many of the portraits in this book can be seen at the Smithsonian Institution's National Portrait Gallery. The mission of the National Portrait Gallery is to tell the story of America by portraying the people who shape the nation's history, development and culture.

The National Portrait Gallery only includes portraits of historical personages, not living people.

T F

Photographs are not included in the National Portrait Gallery.

T F

The stamps included in this book are collected by the National Postal Musuem. The Museum's galleries explore America's postal history and **philately** from colonial times to the present.

The National Portrait Gallery has the nation's only complete collection of presidential portraits outside the White House.

T F

Who was John Wesley Powell?

EXPLORER

DOCTOR

INVENTOR

Who is this man?

JOHN PAUL JONES, NAVAL HERO

DAVID RITTENHOUSE, SCIENTIST

JOHNS HOPKINS, PHILANTHROPIST

What name did Isabella Van Wagener take later in life?

SOJOURNER TRUTH

HARRIET TUBMAN

BESSIE SMITH

COLONISTS AND REVOLUTIONARIES

When the Seven Years' War ended in 1763, the French had lost their bid for empire in the New World. The British and Spanish still held vast and seemingly secure colonial dominions. Within two decades, however, Britain would lose its thirteen colonies and a new nation, the United States of America, would emerge.

BENJAMIN FRANKLIN
1706–1790

Benjamin Franklin returned from his years representing colonial interests in England just in time to be unanimously elected to represent Pennsylvania in the Second Continental Congress. He would later be a signer of the Declaration of Independence. At the close of the Revolutionary War, Franklin was one of the diplomats chosen to negotiate peace with Great Britain and then, as a member of the Constitutional Convention of 1787.

JOHN DICKINSON
1732–1808

John Dickinson's *Letters from a Farmer in Pennsylvania* were published in nineteen of the twenty-three colonial newspapers, and his reasoned case against British taxation made him the first of America's celebrated patriots.

THE ARTICLES OF CONFEDERATION

While Thomas Jefferson drafted the Declaration of Independence, members of the Continental Congress debated and developed a new form of government for the thirteen colonies.

THOMAS MCKEAN

1734–1817

Delaware's enthusiastic signer of the Declaration of Independence also served on the Continental Congress. He was its president when General George Washington marched to Yorktown.

RICHARD HENRY LEE

1732–1794

On June 7, 1776, Richard Henry Lee rose in the Continental Congress to offer a resolution that "these United Colonies are, and of right ought to be, free and independent States," In the wake of those words, the Declaration of Independence became a reality.

MOLLY PITCHER

1754–1832

Mary Ludwig followed her husband, William Hayes, when he enlisted in the Revolutionary army. Ludwig earned her nickname Molly Pitcher by bringing pitchers of water to soldiers in battle. On June 28, 1778, William Hayes participated in the Battle of Monmouth, the longest battle of the war. When he was unable to continue firing his cannon, Mary stepped in and manned the gun through the battle.

SYBIL LUDINGTON

1761–1839

Sybil Ludington rode through the night to call the American militia to arms in defense of liberty. On the night of April 26, 1777, word reached the home of Sybil Ludington that the British were burning Danbury, Connecticut, a nearby town. At age sixteen, she rode her horse on a midnight ride to alert the Minutemen that British Redcoats were burning Danbury.

WHO SAID IT?

THOMAS PAINE

NATHAN HALE

ABIGAIL ADAMS

PATRICK HENRY

MAINTAINING A HERITAGE

American Indian political, economic and cultural life, founded in ancient tradition and tested by wars and removals, has proven its endurance into the 21st century. One key to this extraordinary resilience is found in the wisdom and bravery of its historic leaders.

POCAHONTAS

c. 1595–1617

The daughter of a Powhatan chieftain, Pocahontas was friendly with the nearby English settlers in Jamestown. She frequently delivered food to the English and worked as an emissary between the groups.

TENSKWATAWA

c. 1775–1836

The Shawnee prophet Tenskwatawa had visions that inspired him to preach against all white intrusion into Indian culture.

SARAH WINNEMUCCA

c. 1844–1891

An able and energetic advocate for Native American rights, Sarah Winnemucca mediated diplomatic exchanges between Paiute leaders and government officials.

OSCEOLA
c. 1804–1838

The Seminole Indians of the Southeast were directly affected by Andrew Jackson's policy of Indian removal. Osceola led the resistance against the federal government in a campaign of guerilla warfare.

RED CLOUD
1822–1909

In 1868, the celebrated Lakota leader forced U.S. authorities to abandon a series of newly constructed forts meant to protect settlers moving across traditional native land in present-day Wyoming. In 1870, Red Cloud would turn to diplomacy to protect his tribe's land base and to ensure its political and cultural independence.

BLACK HAWK
1767–1838

Black Hawk led a long resistance to the United States, from fighting on the side of the British during the War of 1812 to instigating what became known as the Black Hawk War in 1832.

TRUE OR FALSE

T F

CHIEF JOSEPH
c. 1840–1904

When U.S. troops were called in to speed the removal process of the Nez Percé people to a reservation in 1877, Joseph and his followers began a strategic retreat, seeking safety first among allied tribes in Montana and then heading toward Canada. They were intercepted only 30 miles from the border and forced to surrender.

GERONIMO
1829–1909

The Apache leader Geronimo resisted all government attempts to confine his people to reservations. "I was born on the prairies where the wind blew free and there was nothing to break the light of the sun. I was born where there were no enclosures."

NELLIE CASHMAN
c. 1849-1925

Cashman, called "The Angel of Tombstone," embodied the adventurous spirit of the West. She emigrated to the U.S. from Ireland in the 1860s and moved West. She earned an honest reputation managing her boarding house in Nevada.

FRONTIERS AND SETTLEMENTS

SACAGAWEA
c. 1788–1812

Sacajawea became one of the most well-known women of the American West through her partnership with Lewis and Clark. As a young Shoshone woman with a child, Sacagawea helped ensure native populations that the group of explorers had peaceful intentions.

JIM BECKWOURTH
c. 1798–1866

During his life as a frontiersman, James P. "Jim" Beckwourth was a miner, guide, fur trapper, company agent, army scout, soldier, and hunter.

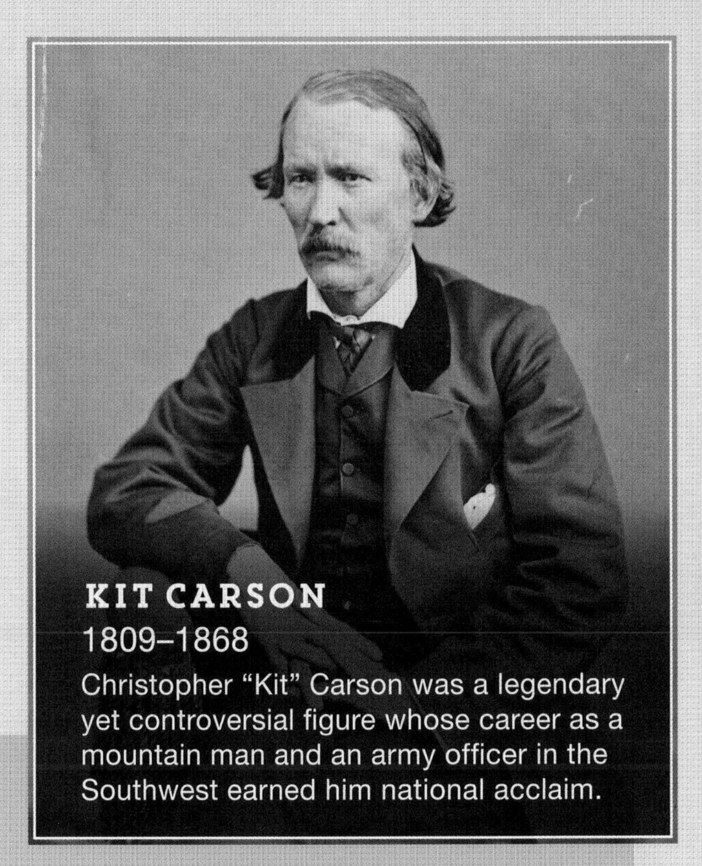

KIT CARSON
1809–1868
Christopher "Kit" Carson was a legendary yet controversial figure whose career as a mountain man and an army officer in the Southwest earned him national acclaim.

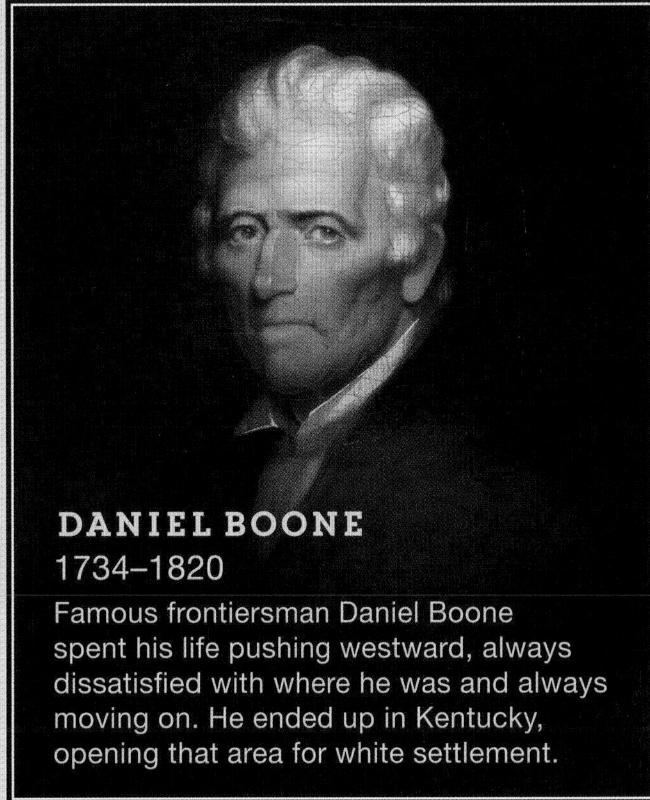

DANIEL BOONE
1734–1820
Famous frontiersman Daniel Boone spent his life pushing westward, always dissatisfied with where he was and always moving on. He ended up in Kentucky, opening that area for white settlement.

WHERE DID THEY GO?

LEARN MORE

JEAN BAPTISTE POINTE DU SABLE
c. 1745–1818
A well-educated sailor from Haiti who lived in France, Jean Baptiste Pointe Du Sable was the first settler and built the first permanent home in an area called Eschikagou, later renamed Chicago.

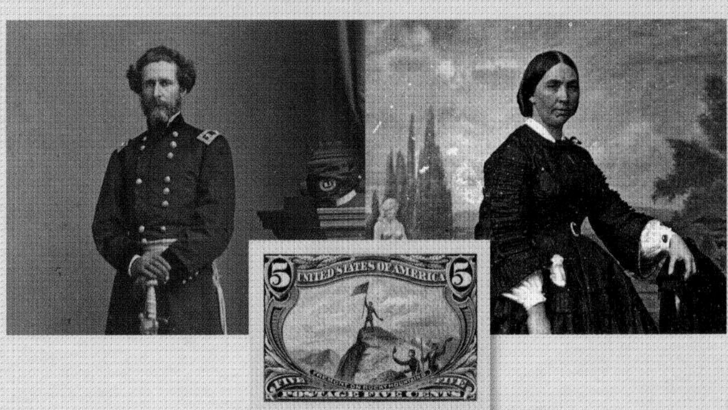

JOHN C. FRÉMONT
1813–1890
JESSIE BENTON FRÉMONT
1824–1902
One of the most famous explorers during a time of the expansionist movement was John C. Frémont. He was in charge of four expeditions in the western territories. His wife Jessie helped him secure funding and collaborated in writing a vivid report of his findings.

JOHN JAMES AUDUBON
1785–1851
Audubon's landmark work, *The Birds of America*, offered the world its hitherto most detailed look at America's diverse species of birds.

CELEBRATING THE WILDERNESS

Throughout America's history, its naturalists, scientists, and authors have shed a spotlight on the natural world and its beauty.

JOHN WESLEY POWELL
1834–1902
John Wesley Powell's work as an explorer, a geologist, and an anthropologist in the American West helped to shape national policies regarding the development of public lands and the welfare of Native American tribes.

LEARN MORE

LAURA INGALLS WILDER

1867–1957

Growing up within a pioneer family herself, Wilder later went on to write the iconic *Little House* children's series that told stories about a family living a pioneer life on the frontier.

JOHN MUIR

1838–1914

Naturalist John Muir spent most of his adult life in California, and a large part of his fame rests on his successful crusade to save California's giant redwoods.

JACK LONDON

1876–1916

Jack London was the most popular and highest paid American writer of his time. London's best-known novels, *The Call of the Wild, White Fang* and *The Sea Wolf,* vividly portray the elemental struggle between man and nature.

EARL SHAFFER

1918–2002

In 1948, Earl Shaffer was the first person to walk the entire Appalachian Trail in one continuous hike. Shaffer had no expert advice, no previous footsteps to follow, or even guidebooks to help him. At the time, experts on the Appalachian Trail believed that a hike of the entire Trail was impossible.

WHO WROTE IT?

NEW FRONTIERS

THE PACIFIC OCEAN:

THE U.S. EXPLORING EXPEDITION

1832–1842

346 MEN

9 SCIENTISTS AND ARTISTS

50,000 PRESSED PLANT SPECIMENS COLLECTED

6 SAILING VESSELS

4,000 ETHNOGRAPHIC ARTIFACTS COLLECTED

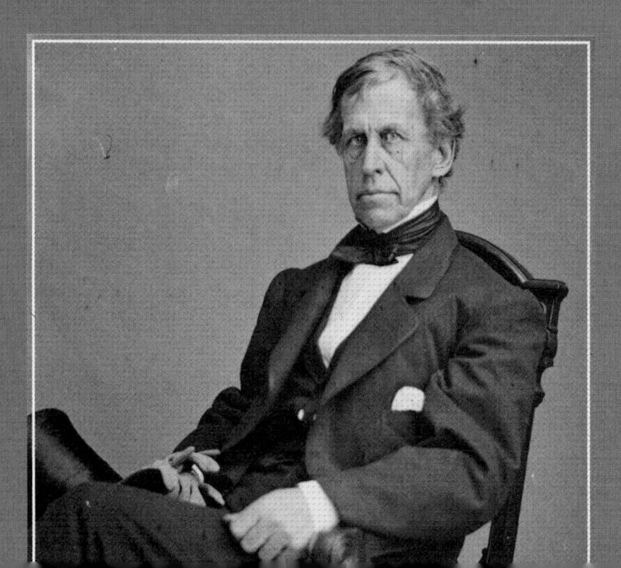

CHARLES WILKES

1798–1877

The head of the expedition was Charles Wilkes, a naval officer and surveyer.

DID THEY GO THERE?

YES NO

ARCTIC EXPLORERS

ELISHA KENT KANE

LEARN MORE

1820–1857

In the 1850s, Elisha Kent Kane's two daring missions in search of missing British explorer Sir John Franklin were the first American-led Arctic expeditions.

ADOLPHUS GREELY

LEARN MORE

1844–1935

Greely's party reached a point that was the closest any explorer had come to the North Pole.

DISCOVERERS OF THE NORTH POLE

Admiral Robert Peary (1856–1920) headed the expedition that discovered the North Pole. Matthew Henson (1866–1955) was the most trusted member of that expedition. Peary and Henson's shared sense of adventure bound them together for more than 20 years. Henson accompanied Peary on several attempts to reach the North Pole, which they finally reached together on April 6, 1909.

ARCTIC EXPLORATIONS 1909 1959 U.S. POSTAGE 4¢

ANTARCTIC EXPLORERS

NATHANIEL B. PALMER
1799–1877

RICHARD BYRD
1888–1957

LINCOLN ELLSWORTH
1880–1951

PRESIDENTS

1 GEORGE WASHINGTON
1732–1799

2 JOHN ADAMS
1735–1826

3 THOMAS JEFFERSON
1743–1826

4 JAMES MADISON
1751–1836

5 JAMES MONROE
1758–1831

6 JOHN QUINCY ADAMS
1767–1848

7 ANDREW JACKSON
1767–1845

8 MARTIN VAN BUREN
1782–1862

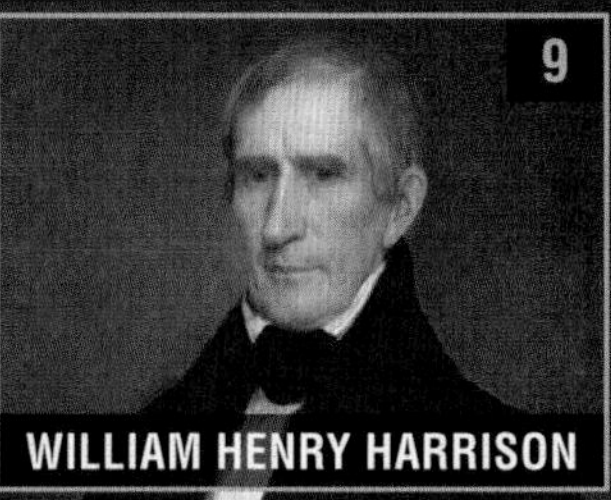
9 WILLIAM HENRY HARRISON
1773–1841

10 JOHN TYLER
1790–1862

11 JAMES K. POLK
1795–1849

12 ZACHARY TAYLOR
1784–1850

13 MILLARD FILLMORE
1800–1874

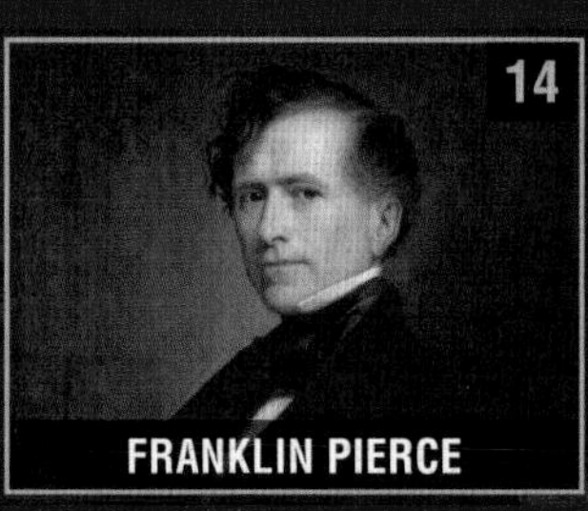
14 FRANKLIN PIERCE
1804–1869

15 JAMES BUCHANAN
1791–1868

16 ABRAHAM LINCOLN
1809–1865

17 ANDREW JOHNSON
1808–1875

18 ULYSSES S. GRANT
1822–1885

19 RUTHERFORD B. HAYES
1822–1893

20 JAMES GARFIELD
1831–1881

BY THE NUMBERS

21
CHESTER ARTHUR
1829–1886
22 & 24
GROVER CLEVELAND
1837–1908
23
BENJAMIN HARRISON
1833–1901
25
WILLIAM MCKINLEY
1843–1901
26
THEODORE ROOSEVELT
1858–1919
27
WILLIAM TAFT
1857–1930
28
WOODROW WILSON
1856–1924
29
WARREN HARDING
1865–1923
30
CALVIN COOLIDGE
1872–1933
31
HERBERT HOOVER
1874–1964
32
FRANKLIN D. ROOSEVELT
1882–1945
33
HARRY TRUMAN
1884–1972
34
DWIGHT EISENHOWER
1890–1969
35
JOHN F. KENNEDY
1917–1963
36
LYNDON B. JOHNSON
1908–1973
37
RICHARD NIXON
1913–1994
38
GERALD FORD
1913–2006
39
JIMMY CARTER
1924–
40
RONALD REAGAN
1911–2004
41
GEORGE H.W. BUSH
1924–
42
WILLIAM CLINTON
43
GEORGE W. BUSH
44
BARACK OBAMA

JOHN JAY
1745–1829
Founding Father John Jay was the first chief justice of the United States.

ALEXANDER HAMILTON
1755–1804
By the time George Washington appointed Hamilton the first secretary of the treasury in 1789, Hamilton had achieved success in war and in marriage, reputation in the law and politics, and fame as the instigator and one of the authors of the *Federalist Papers*.

SERVING A GROWING NATION

Alongside the nation's presidents, the country has been served by its cabinet members, representatives, jurists, and others.

JOHN MARSHALL
1755–1835
John Marshall, appointed by John Adams, served as the chief justice for more than three decades, firmly establishing the judiciary as a coequal branch of the government."

DOLLEY MADISON

1768–1849

Dolley Madison's courage and charisma represent hallmarks of a First Lady. She accompanied her husband, James Madison, to Washington, D.C., when he served as Secretary of State under President Jefferson. Her political knowledge and social skills greatly assisted Jefferson and he asked her to serve as his official hostess in the White House. Dolley continued as hostess when Madison became President.

JUSTIN MORRILL

1810–1898

Congressman Justin Morrill is widely remembered for sponsoring the Morrill Acts of 1862 and 1890 to establish land-grant colleges.

DANIEL WEBSTER

1782–1852

In a period when American federalism faced increasing challenges from states'-rights supporters, Daniel Webster emerged as one of the Union's most eloquent defenders.

FIRSTS AND RECORDS

WILLIAM DOUGLAS

JOHN DINGELL

THOMAS JEFFERSON

OLIVER WENDELL HOLMES, JR.

FREDERICK MUHLENBERG

SHAPING THE HALLS OF POWER

The 20th century brought new diversity to the federal government. Here were some of the trailblazers.

MARGARET CHASE SMITH

1897–1995

Smith was the first Republican woman elected to the U.S. Senate and the first woman to serve in both houses of Congress.

HATTIE CARRAWAY

1878–1950

Carraway was the first woman elected to the U.S. Senate.

ELEANOR ROOSEVELT

1884–1962

Roosevelt demonstrated how women could redefine traditional roles and create a new place in American culture. Eleanor created a long legacy that extended far beyond her years as First Lady. She redefined the role of a First Lady, becoming an activist and world leader in her own right.

FRANCES PERKINS

1880–1965

Perkins was the first female member of a presidential cabinet, serving as secretary of labor for Franklin D. Roosevelt.

LEARN MORE

THURGOOD MARSHALL

1908–1993

Marshall made history in 1967, when he was sworn in as the first African-American justice of the U.S. Supreme Court.

The Plaintiffs of *Mendez et al.*

In 1945, a group of Hispanic parents in California filed suit to end segregation in their schools. The ground-breaking case, *Mendez et al. v. Westminster School District et al.*, was decided in 1947 when the 9th Circuit Court of Appeals in San Francisco ruled that the school districts could not segregate on the basis of national origin.

LEARN MORE

DENNIS CHAVEZ

1888–1962

As a United States senator, Dennis Chavez fought for the rights of Hispanic residents and Native Americans in his home state of New Mexico.

IN THE YEAR...

1935 1944 1954

1940 1946

REVOLUTIONARY WAR HEROES

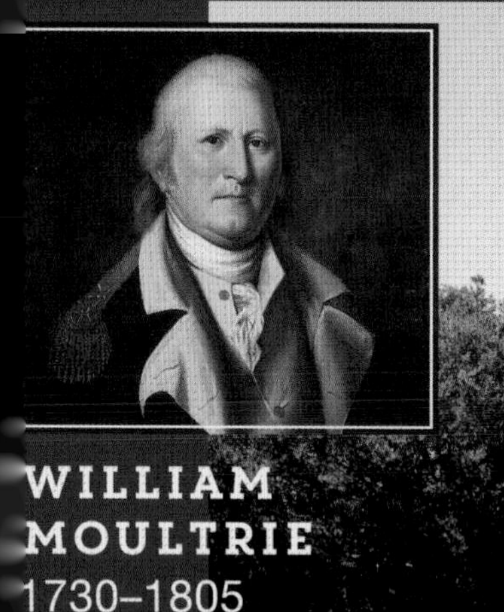

WILLIAM MOULTRIE
1730–1805

HENRY KNOX
1750–1806

DEFENDERS

JOHN PAUL JONES
1747–1792

PIRATE FIGHTER!

STEPHEN DECATUR
1779–1820

CIVIL WAR STALWARTS

JOHN ERICSSON
1803–1889

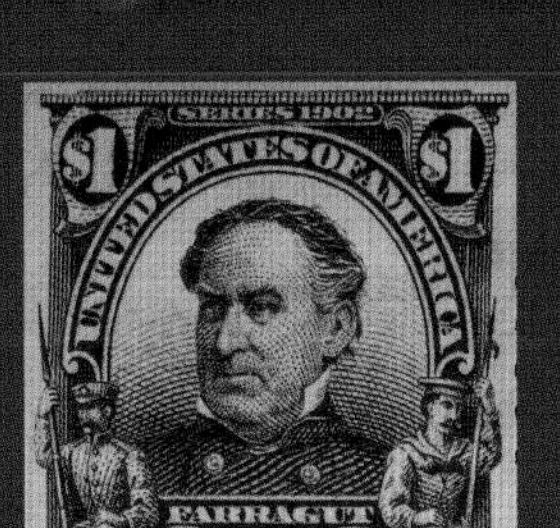

DAVID FARRAGUT
1801–1870

ULYSSES S. GRANT
1822–1885

WORLD WAR II LEADERS

CHESTER NIMITZ
1885–1966

HENRY HARLEY "HAP" ARNOLD
1886–1950

GEORGE C. MARSHALL
1880–1959

QUOTABLE QUOTES

Damn the torpedoes! Full speed ahead!

I can't spare this man —he fights.

Our country, right or wrong.

I have not yet begun to fight.

REFORMERS

Many Americans have had ideas, often contradictory, about what would make America better. The people on these pages had the drive to try to turn their visions into reality.

BENJAMIN LAY
c. 1681–1759

Quaker reformer Benjamin Lay was a key figure in the emerging antislavery movement prior to the Revolutionary War. Having witnessed slavery's horrors while working as a merchant in Barbados, Lay dedicated himself to the abolitionist cause.

HORACE MANN
1796–1859

Mann worked to reform education. Free public education, he proclaimed, was essential, at a time of increased immigration and expanding democracy, to the good order and prosperity of society.

JOHN QUINCY ADAMS
1767–1848

Adams served an undistinguished presidency, and was viewed as rigid, humorless, and out of step. But in his life's second act, he returned to Congress in 1831 and became known as "Old Man Eloquent" for his passionate opposition to slavery.

PADRE FÉLIX VARELA

1788–1853

In the early 1820s, Padre Félix Varela concentrated his efforts on helping poor minorities living in New York City and founded nurseries and orphanages for the children of poor widows. He organized the New York Temperance Association and lived in hospitals while caring for cholera victims during an epidemic in 1832.

WILLIAM LLOYD GARRISON

1805–1879

Single-handedly, William Lloyd Garrison transformed the antislavery movement from a discussion about gradually ending slavery into a moral crusade demanding "immediate and complete emancipation." A printer and editor, Garrison experienced his near-religious conversion to abolitionism around 1828 and founded the American Anti-Slavery Society in 1833.

DOROTHEA DIX

1802–1887

In 1841, teacher, humanitarian, and reformer Dorothea Dix launched a vigorous campaign to secure humane treatment for the mentally ill. At a time when such individuals were more often imprisoned and abused than cared for and treated, Dix became a tireless advocate for their welfare.

HENRY GEORGE

1839–1897

As American industry after the Civil War spawned undreamed-of wealth for some and a new and excruciating poverty for others, economist Henry George became a leading voice in efforts to reform the nation's free-enterprise system.

TRUE OR FALSE T F

BELVA ANN LOCKWOOD

1830–1917

Lockwood worked to expand the rights of women. Barred later from utilizing a hard-won law degree in many courts, she lobbied for a congressional bill permitting women to argue before the Supreme Court and, on its passage in 1879, became the first woman admitted to practice in that tribunal.

CHARLOTTE PERKINS GILMAN

1860–1935

During an age when social conventions limited the opportunities for women, author Charlotte Perkins Gilman was influential in exposing the problems that lay behind the sentimental facade of domesticity.

UPTON SINCLAIR

1878–1968

Upton Sinclair published *The Jungle*—one of the most influential novels of its day in 1906. Intending to expose corruption and wretched conditions for workers, Sinclair had spent seven weeks living in Chicago's meatpacking district. But *The Jungle* also revealed the appalling sanitary conditions of the industry.

JANE ADDAMS

1860–1935

Jane Addams led the field of social work from her settlement house located in an immigrant community in Chicago, Illinois. She sought to solve the problems of industrial America through social reform.

ALICE HAMILTON, M.D.

1869–1970

Dr. Alice Hamilton spent 22 years in Chicago as a resident at Jane Addams' Hull House, where her eyes were opened to the problems of the working class in industrialized America. Her 1911 study conclusively demonstrated the prevalence of lead poisoning in industry, leading to measurable improvements in many factories.

CESAR CHAVEZ

1927–1993

Cesar E. Chavez founded the United Farm Workers of America, AFL-CIO (UFW). He was a tireless advocate for nonviolent social change.

WHO SAID IT?

FROM SLAVERY TO FREEDOM

Some of the most powerful words, stories, and images of the abolitionist movement came from people who had themselves been slaves.

OLAUDAH EQUIANO

1745–1797

"Permit me, with the greatest deference and respect, to lay at your feet the following genuine Narrative; the chief design of which is to excite in your august assemblies a sense of compassion for the miseries which the Slave-Trade has entailed on my unfortunate countrymen."
—*The Interesting Narrative of the Life of Olaudah Equiano, Or Gustavus Vassa, The African, Written By Himself*

SOJOURNER TRUTH

c. 1797–1883

"That man over there says that women need to be helped into carriages, and lifted over ditches, and to have the best place everywhere. Nobody ever helps me into carriages, or over mud-puddles, or gives me any best place! And ain't I a woman? Look at me! Look at my arm! I have ploughed and planted, and gathered into barns, and no man could head me! And ain't I a woman? I could work as much and eat as much as a man—when I could get it —and bear the lash as well! And ain't I a woman?"
—Speech delivered in 1851 at Women's Rights Convention, Akron, Ohio

HARRIET TUBMAN

c. 1820–1913

"The midnight sky and the silent stars have been the witnesses of your devotion to freedom and of your heroism. Excepting John Brown—of sacred memory—I know of no one who has willingly encountered more perils and hardships to serve our enslaved people than you have."
—Frederick Douglass, letter to Harriet Tubman, 1868

FREDERICK DOUGLASS

1818–1895

"In the early part of the year 1838, I became quite restless. I could see no reason why I should, at the end of each week, pour the reward of my toil into the purse of my master. When I carried to him my weekly wages, he would, after counting the money, look me in the face with a robber-like fierceness, and ask, 'Is this all?' He was satisfied with nothing less than the last cent. He would, however, when I made him six dollars, sometimes give me six cents, to encourage me. It had the opposite effect. I regarded it as a sort of admission of my right to the whole."
Narrative of the Life of Frederick Douglass, an American Slave

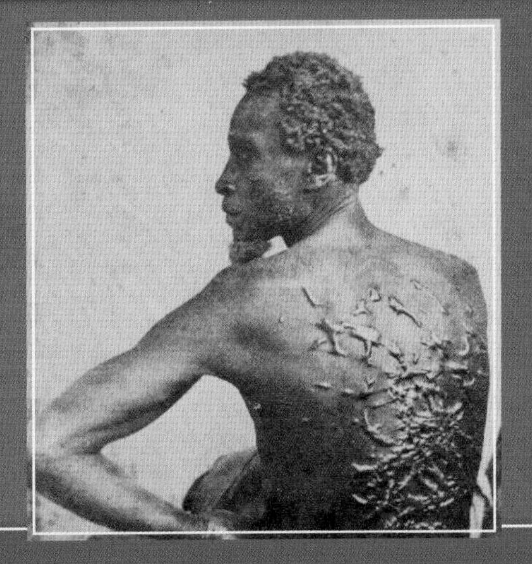

GORDON

dates unknown

"This Card Photograph should be multiplied by 100,000 and scattered over the States. It tells the story in a way that even Mrs. [Harriet Beecher] Stowe can not approach, because it tells the story to the eye."
—Contemporary journalist

THE CONTINUED STRUGGLE

The struggle for equality for African Americans did not end with slavery. In the generations that followed, black Americans fought for economic equality, the right to vote, and the end to discrimination.

IDA B. WELLS

1862–1931

Born a slave in 1862, Ida B. Wells devoted her entire life to educating people about the horrors of discrimination and lynching.

W.E.B. DU BOIS

1868–1963

Sociologist and historian W.E.B. Du Bois originated the policies—legal suits, legislative lobbying, and public protest—that characterized the civil rights movement of the 1950s and 1960s. He is often called the "father of social science" for his trail-blazing approach to studying social systems and phenomena.

A. PHILIP RANDOLPH

1889 –1979

Civil rights activist A. Philip Randolph waged a lifelong battle for the economic empowerment of African Americans. In 1925 he accepted the challenge of organizing the Brotherhood of Sleeping Car Porters—the first black labor union chartered by the American Federation of Labor.

FANNIE LOU HAMER

1917 –1977

Hamer was a Mississippi sharecropper who fought for black voting rights and spoke for many when she said, "I'm sick and tired of being sick and tired."

MEDGAR EVERS

1925 –1963

Evers served with distinction as an official of the NAACP in Mississippi until his assassination in 1963.

LEARN MORE ABOUT MARTIN LUTHER KING, JR.

ROY WILKINS

1901–1981

In 1931, Wilkins was appointed assistant executive secretary of the National Association for the Advancement of Colored People (NAACP), the largest civil rights organization in the United States. In 1955, he was named the NAACP's executive secretary, a position he held for the next 22 years.

MARTIN LUTHER KING, JR.

929–1968

Martin Luther King, Jr. was the most powerful nd popular leader of the African-American rotest movement of the 1950s and 1960s. He pearheaded mass action through marches, sit-s, boycotts, and nonviolent demonstrations hat profoundly and positively affected America's ttitudes toward racial prejudice and discrimination.

QUICK QUIZ

A B

MALCOLM X

1925–1965

Malcolm X emerged in the 1950s as a major spokesperson for African Americans. He became a leader in the Nation of Islam. He initially advocated separatism for blacks in America, but then split from th Nation of Islam and sought to unify all blacks to work

CHRONICLERS AND RECORDERS

WILLIAM HICKLING PRESCOTT

1796–1859

The first major American historian

His works include:

The History of Ferdinand and Isabella
The History of the Conquest of Mexico
The History of the Conquest of Peru

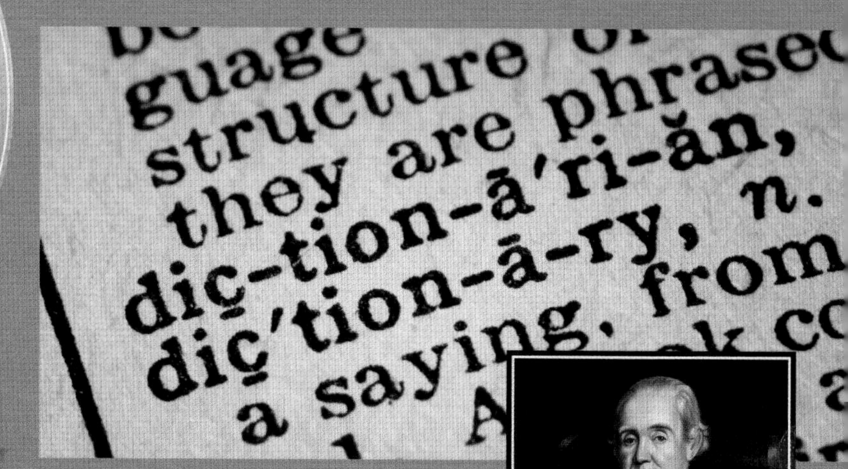

NOAH WEBSTER

1758–1843

Lexicographer

JOHN RUSSWURM

1799–1851

Co-editor of the first black newspaper in the U.S.

SARAH JOSEPHA BUELL HALE

1788–1879

Literary editor

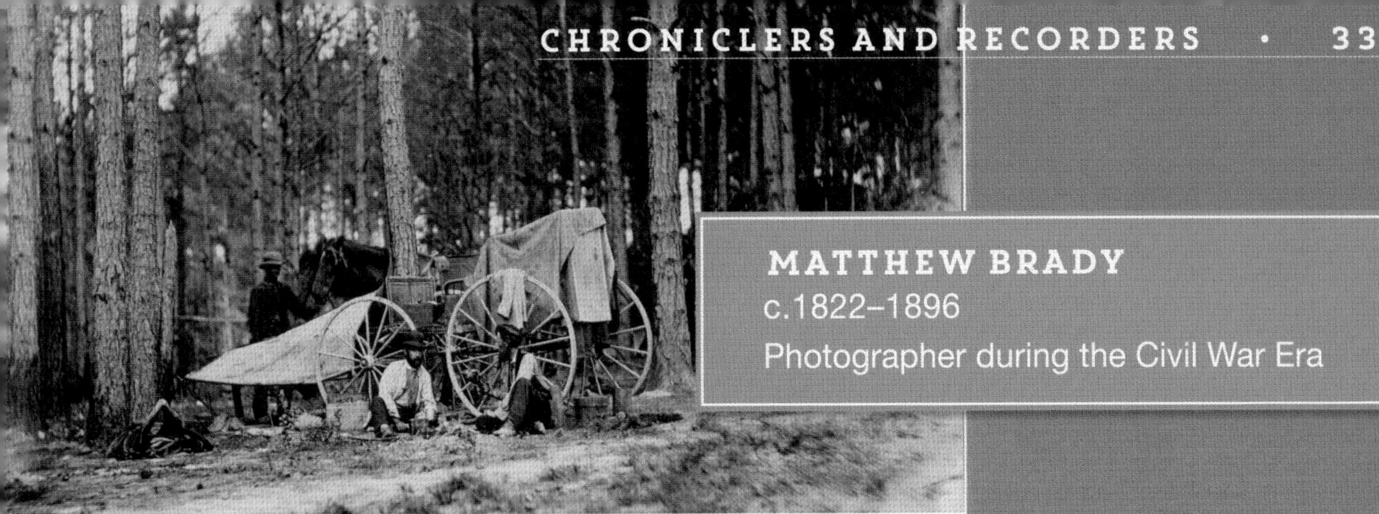

MATTHEW BRADY
c.1822–1896
Photographer during the Civil War Era

HORACE GREELEY
1811–1872
Founder and editor, *New York Tribune*; social reformer

NELLIE BLY
1864–1922
Investigative journalist

IDA TARBELL
1857–1944
Investigative journalist

LEARN MORE

MARGUERITE HIGGINS
1920–1966
War correspondent

ERNEST "ERNIE" T. PYLE
1900–1945
War correspondent

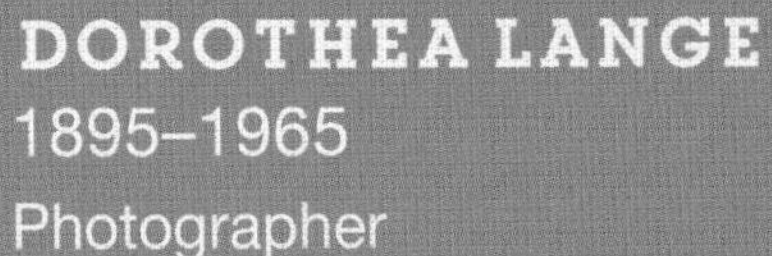

DOROTHEA LANGE
1895–1965
Photographer

WHO WROTE IT?

EARLY AMERICAN WRITERS

PHILLIS WHEATLEY

1753–1784

Phillis Wheatley was the first African American to publish a book and the first American woman to earn a living from her writing. This was no small feat, considering that she came to America as a slave.

WASHINGTON IRVING

1783–1859

Trained as a lawyer, Washington Irving found the law tedious and drifted into writing. He became a popular and critical success in both America and England with such tales as "Rip Van Winkle" and "The Legend of Sleepy Hollow."

HARRIET BEECHER STOWE

1811–1896

Excluded from public professions, cultivated women sought other avenues for their talents. From discussing the issues of the day in informal salon gatherings, it was a short step for women to become writers, especially since the **antebellum period** saw a burgeoning number of magazines catering to women. So Harriet Beecher Stowe started a career that made her one of the most popular novelists of the nineteenth century

HENRY WADSWORTH LONGFELLOW

1807–1882

As a poet, Henry Wadsworth Longfellow has suffered the fate of many popular writers: a voice of its time frequently lacks staying power. Nonetheless, he was the country's first professional poet because he had the literary knowledge and craftsmanship necessary to write verse about America that was comparable in quality to that of his English contemporaries.

NATHANIEL HAWTHORNE

1804–1864

Nathaniel Hawthorne drew upon his knowledge of both family and local history to create the plots and settings for such highly regarded works as *The Scarlet Letter* (1850) and *The House of the Seven Gables* (1851).

RALPH WALDO EMERSON

1803–1882

In his voluminous writings, Emerson created a uniquely American school of philosophy. Emerson preached self-reliance as Americans' core attribute; this empowered the individual in a way that led to dreams of perfectionism and supported the culture of American business.

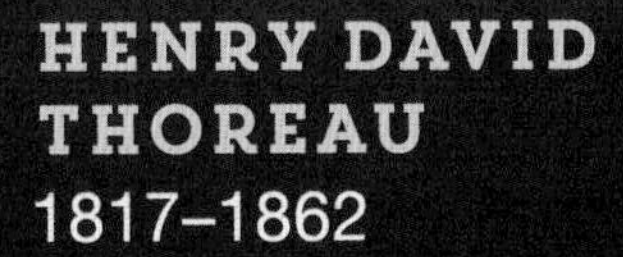

HENRY DAVID THOREAU

1817–1862

Described by a contemporary as "the apostle of individuality in an age of association and compromise," author Henry David Thoreau followed his own moral compass and lived a life largely unfettered by convention.

LOUISA MAY ALCOTT

1832–1888

Asked by her publisher to write a book for girls, Alcott drew upon her own family experiences to write *Little Women* (1868). This heartwarming novel, chronicling the lives of the four March sisters—Meg, Jo, Beth, and Amy—was a success at its publication and remains an American literary classic.

WALT WHITMAN

1819–1892

Whitman was one of the few poets of his era to depart from a conservative style, making frequent use of rambling blank verse and free verse.

FAMOUS FIRST LINES

"The Song of Hiawatha"

Little Women

The Scarlet Letter

Uncle Tom's Cabin

BUILDING A LITERARY TRADITION

SAMUEL CLEMENS

1835–1910

Using the pen name Mark Twain, Samuel Clemens had become one of this country's favorite satiric writers by the early 1870s, routinely making light of everyday human foibles. But it was the publication of *The Adventures of Tom Sawyer* (1876) and *The Adventures of Huckleberry Finn* (1884) that assured him a lasting place in American letters.

PAUL LAURENCE DUNBAR

1872–1906

Although Dunbar wrote three novels and many short stories, it was his poetry, written in both standard English and African American dialect, that first caught the attention of a national audience and allowed him to leave his job as an elevator operator.

EMILY DICKINSON

1830–1886

Though considered by many the greatest American female poet of the nineteenth century, Dickinson saw only a few of her 1,700 poems published in her lifetime, and those were published anonymously and without her permission.

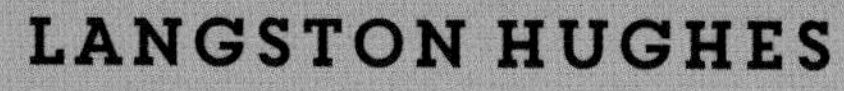

LANGSTON HUGHES

1902–1967

Although he was considered a poet first, Hughes wrote in many literary genres, ranging from short stories to drama.

EUGENE O'NEILL

1888–1953

Playwright Eugene O'Neill's melodramas, musicals, and farces transformed the American theatre into a serious literary medium.

LEARN MORE

JAMES BALDWIN

1924–1987

As one of the most passionate and eloquent writers about the problems of race in America, Baldwin gave substantial impetus to the civil rights ferment of the 1950s and 1960s.

EDNA ST. VINCENT MILLAY

1892–1950

In 1923, Edna St. Vincent Millay became the first woman to win the Pulitzer Prize for poetry.

EDITH WHARTON

1862–1937

Wharton became famous for her critical depictions of the New York upper class, as in the Pulitzer Prize-winning *Age of Innocence*.

ZORA NEALE HURSTON

1891–1960

American writer, folklorist, and anthropologist Zora Neale Hurston was one of America's most original and accomplished writers and a central figure in the **Harlem Renaissance**. Her best known novel is *Their Eyes Were Watching God* (1937).

CLOSING LINES

The Adventures of Huckleberry Finn

Go Tell It on the Mountain

The Age of Innocence

Their Eyes Were Watching God

ROBERT FROST

1874–1963

Over his long, calculated, and prize-winning career as America's best-loved poet, Robert Frost became the epitome of the New England Yankee: a weathered, craggy, flinty, and plainspoken countryman who turned ordinary life into poetry.

MUSICIANS

IN THE 1800S

In 1871, in an effort to raise funds for the Fisk University, a newly founded African American school in Nashville, Tennessee, a student singing group was formed, soon to be called the Fisk Jubilee Singers. The group, composed mostly of former slaves, became instantly popular, and their concert tours were soon raising substantial amounts of money.

TERESA CARREÑO

1853–1917

Pianist Teresa Carreño was only eight years old and a recent émigré from Venezuela when she gave her first public recital in New York in 1862. This debut was a resounding success. Within a year, she was performing for President Lincoln at the White House.

ISABELLA HINCKLEY

1840–1862

Soprano Isabella Hinckley was one of the first Americans to win critical acclaim as an operatic performer. She began her singing career in her early teens.

LEARN MORE

THE CARTER FAMILY

Sara Dougherty Carter (1898–1979) and Maybelle Carter (1909–1978) were cousins that formed their own country music group, The Carter Family. The third musician within the group was Maybelle Carter's husband, Alvin P. Carter (1891–1960).

PATSY CLINE

1932–1963

Cline greatly contributed to the popularization of country music across America.

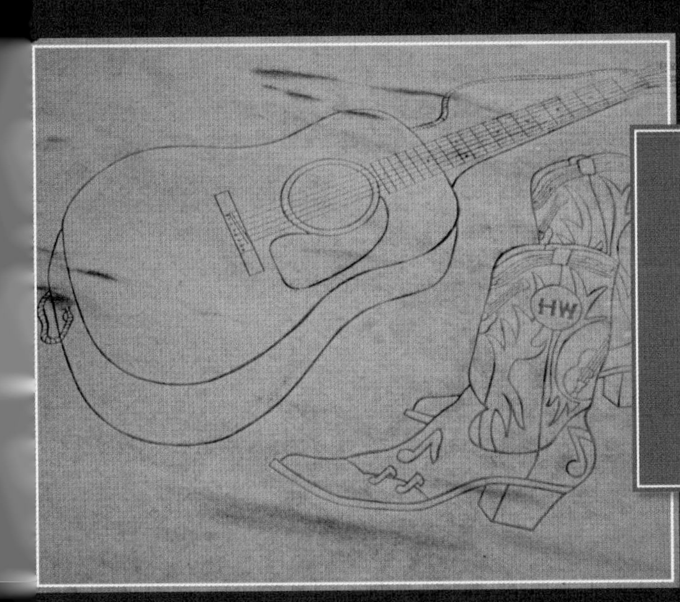

HANK WILLIAMS

1923–1953

After a few years in the violent honky-tonks of the Deep South, Williams and his band, the Drifting Cowboys, began to perform songs about the hard-won dignities of the country's rural past for the newly urbanized masses of the late 1940s.

JAZZ AND BLUES

LOUIS ARMSTRONG

1901–1971

His unique brand of improvising and "scat" singing gave Armstrong multifaceted appeal that landed him roles in films, on radio, and later in television. This early style of jazz vocalizing involved imitating the sounds and phrases of the instrument. With his deep range and raspy vocal quality, Armstrong switched from trumpet to voice in such classics as "What a Wonderful World" and "Hello Dolly."

LEGENDS

DUKE ELLINGTON

ROBERT JOHNSON

BESSIE SMITH

BILLIE HOLIDAY

FOR:

SING, SING, SING,

STOMPIN' AT THE SAVOY

DON'T BE THAT WAY

BENNY GOODMAN

1909–1986

Bandleader Goodman was known as the "King of Swing." He also played the clarinet.

KNOWN FOR:

ONE O'CLOCK JUMP

JUMPIN' AT THE WOODSIDE

COUNT BASIE

1904–1984

Born William Basie, "The Count" was a renowned jazz pianist, bandleader, and composer. His band included some of the greate musicians of all time.

KNOWN FOR:

MOONLIGHT SERENADE

GLENN MILLER

1904–1944

(Missing in Action)

The swing music the Miller and his orchestra performed was infused with elements of azz and featured a unique combination of sound rom the clarinet and saxophone. The bandleader's oure, romantic swing sound appealed to dance audiences nationally and overseas.

CLASSIC BROADWAY TEAM

WHO COMPOSED THE SONGS?

WHO WROTE THE LYRICS?

GEORGE GERSHWIN

1898–1937

IRA GERSHWIN

1896–1983

The Gershwin brothers collaborated on many projects, including the folk opera *Porgy and Bess.*

ALAN JAY LERNER

1918–1986

FREDERICK LOEWE

1901–1988

Lerner and Loewe's most famous works incl *My Fair Lady, Brigadoon, and Camelot.*

RICHARD RODGERS

1902–1979

OSCAR HAMMERSTEIN II

1895–1960

Rodgers and Hammerstein created such classics as *Oklahoma!,* *King and I, and The Sound of Music*

PIONEERS OF ROCK & ROLL

KNOWN FOR:

COME ON, LET'S GO

DONNA

LA BAMBA

RITCHIE VALENS

1941–1959

In an all too brief career, Latin rock and rhythm composer and singer Ritchie Valens was the first Chicano rock and roll star.

BUDDY HOLLY

1936–1959

Born Charles Hardin Holley, Holly played several instruments, including guitar and piano.

KNOWN FOR:

THAT'LL BE THE DAY

PEGGY SUE

EVERYDAY

ELVIS PRESLEY

1935–1977

Elvis Presley released hundreds of records throughout a career that spanned slightly more than two decades. He also starred in thirty-one feature films and two documentaries.

SIGNATURE SONG

FOLK SINGERS

WOODY GUTHRIE

JOSH WHITE

SONNY TERRY

LEADBELLY

ON STAGE AND SCREEN

In the 1800s, the fledgling country was still striving to establish its cultural independence from Europe. This page shows some of the legendary actors and actresses who established an American stage tradition.

JAMES HENRY HACKETT

1800–1871

A character actor who specialized in comic American "types," James Henry Hackett made his debut in 1826. Here he is shown in the role of Rip Van Winkle, in a play he adapted in 1830 from Washington Irving's story.

EDWIN FORREST

1806–1872

The creator of a distinctly American school of acting, Edwin Forrest made his New York debut in Othello in 1826 at the age of twenty and for many years enjoyed an unrivaled popularity with the American public.

IRA ALDRIDGE

1807–1867

The career of Ira Aldridge illustrates the costs that racism inflicted on African Americans and on America itself. Aldridge was one of the great actors of his age—but he was black. Unable to work in America, he moved to England in the 1820s and lived abroad until his death.

CHARLOTTE CUSHMAN

1816–1876

Charlotte Cushman debuted as Lady Macbeth in 1836 and thereafter went from strength to strength in a range of widely praised performances. She exemplified the vigor, passion, and emotional fervor that were prized both by the Romantics and by Americans eager to assert their cultural distinctiveness from Europe.

KATE BATEMAN

1842–1917

Just four years old when she made her acting debut, Kate Bateman enjoyed great success as a child prodigy until she outgrew such roles at the age of fourteen and briefly retired from the stage. She reemerged in 1860 in the title role of *Evangeline*, a dramatization of Henry Wadsworth Longfellow's celebrated poem.

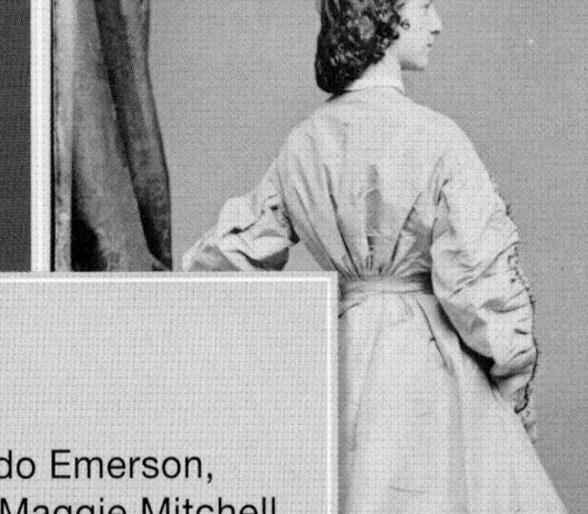

MAGGIE MITCHELL

1832–1918

A winsome actress who counted Abraham Lincoln, Ralph Waldo Emerson, and Henry Wadsworth Longfellow among her many admirers, Maggie Mitchell parlayed the title role in *Fanchon*, the *Cricket*, into the mainstay of her career.

THE SILENT STARS

In the early days of film, before "talkies" had been invented, all movies were silent. Despite the lack of sound, talented silent film stars conveyed a variety of characters and emotions through acting.

CHARLIE CHAPLIN | RUDOLPH VALENTINO | ZASU PITTS | THEDA BARA | CLARA BOW | LON CHANEY | BUSTER KEATON

STARRING ROLE

ARTISTS

From the early colonial period to the present day, American artists have captured their interpretation of the American experience using different forms of art.

GILBERT STUART

1755–1828

Self-portrait

Following the early success of his painting "The Skater," Stuart established a studio in Philadelphia, where he created numerous portraits of the nation's Founding Fathers. He is best known for his portraits of George Washington, including the iconic "Athenaeum Head" that appears on the dollar bill.

JOHN SINGLETON COPLEY

1738–1815

Self-portrait

John Singleton Copley, proclaimed John Adams, is "the greatest Master, that ever was in America." While still a teenager, Copley was capable of satisfying Bostonians' desire for realistic portraits; by the time he was twenty, the essentially self-taught artist was painting better pictures than he had ever seen.

JOHN TRUMBULL

1756–1843

Detail from the *Declaration of Independence*

Trumbull produced a monumental painting of the signing of the Declaration of Independence. Trumbull painted forty-two of the fifty-six signers of the Declaration and used real life models and sittings to capture the details of the delegates.

WINSLOW HOMER

1836–1910

Four Rowboats with Children

Landscape painter Winslow Homer loved the sea, and he brilliantly depicted its qualities.

FREDERIC REMINGTON

1861–1909

The Bronco Buster

Remington, an American painter, author, and sculptor, was noted for his realistic portrayals of the "Old West." His work documented and captured the spirit of the American frontier, both historically and geographically.

JAMES MCNEILL WHISTLER

1834–1903

Study for self-portrait

Whistler's style was subtle, often producing what he called 'arrangements' or 'nocturnes' in just two colors. Better known works include "At the Piano," "Symphony in White, No.1: The White Girl," and his principal effort in decorative art, "Peacock Room."

CECILIA BEAUX

1855–1942

Self-portrait

The first woman hired to teach at the renowned Pennsylvania Academy of the Fine Arts, Beaux became one of the most admired portraitists of her generation. Beaux received a gold medal from the American Academy of Arts and Letters for lifetime achievement, and she was one of the first Americans invited to contribute a self-portrait to the Uffizi collection in Florence.

MARY CASSATT

1844–1926

Self-portrait

Cassatt used her art to address the many roles of the modern woman-as mother, as intellectual, and here, as professional artist.

WHICH ARTIST?

THRIVING TRADITIONS

American art continued to grow and change in the 20th and throughout the present day.

WHAT DID NORMAN ROCKWELL PAINT IN THIS BOOK?

NORMAN ROCKWELL

1894–1978

Rockwell, the well-known illustrator of *Saturday Evening Post* covers beginning in 1916 at the age of twenty-two, serves as a prime example of an artist who used his art to honor 'main street' America.

ISAMU NOGUCHI

1904–1988

Isamu Noguchi garnered international acclaim as a versatile sculptor who created evocative works in media ranging from stone and steel to clay and paper.

GRANT WOOD

1891–1942

Wood was born in Iowa and lived in the Midwest for his entire life. He was a supporter of the Regionalist Movement, a style of painting that focused on rural life and traditional American values.

ANSEL ADAMS

1902–1984

Renowned landscape photographer Ansel Adams is known for his detailed images of the American West.

EDWARD HOPPER

1882–1967

Born in New York, Hopper is regarded as one of America's greatest scene painters. He often painted scenes that illustrated alienation and isolated individuals in modern settings.

WHICH MOVEMENT?

REGIONALIST

ASH CAN

ABSTRACT EXPRESSIONISM

HUDSON RIVER

SCIENTISTS

American scientists have made contributions that have advanced scientific knowledge not only in America, but globally.

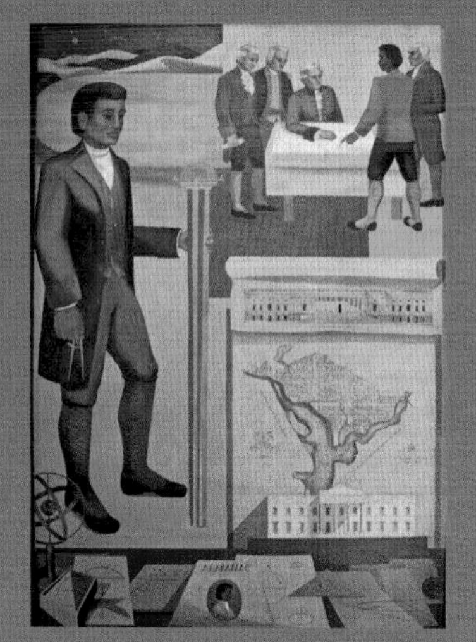

BENJAMIN BANNEKER

1731–1806

A surveyor, astronomer, mathematician and craftsman, Benjamin Banneker was a member of the surveying team that laid out the plans for the new capitol, Washington, D.C.

DAVID RITTENHOUSE

1732–1796

A clockmaker by trade and a self-taught mathematician and astronomer, Rittenhouse was one of the foremost men of science in the eighteenth century.

NATHANIEL BOWDITCH

1773–1838

The self-taught Bowditch was the leading American scientist during the first three decades of the nineteeth century. His contributions to navigation and astronomy were signal achievements in the new republic, helping to create an identity distinct from England.

LEARN MORE

JOSIAH WILLARD GIBBS

1839–1903

One of the great theoretical scientists of his age, J. Willard Gibbs worked out of Yale University.

GEORGE WASHINGTON CARVER

c. 1864–1943

Carver overcame racial prejudice to complete his education in agriculture and botany. As an agricultural chemist, he developed a multitude of industrial uses for common crops such as peanuts, soybeans, and sweet potatoes.

LEARN MORE

RACHEL CARSON

1907–1964

Carson's groundbreaking 1962 book *Silent Spring* sparked a controversy regarding the dangerous effects of pesticides. She testified before Congress and called for improved ecological awareness, helping promote the environmental movement of the late 20th century.

LEARN MORE

RICHARD FEYNMAN

1918–1988

Feynman was one of the winners of the 1965 Nobel Prize on Physics for his work in quantum electrodynamics.

ROBERT MILLIKAN

1868–1953

Millikan made many significant contributions to the twentieth-century revolution in Physics. He was best known for his research on cosmic rays, which he named.

BARBARA MCCLINTOCK

1902–1992

McClintock pursued genetics research, focusing on maize (corn) genetics. She researched the suppression and expression of certain genetic traits from one generation to another and developed theories that linked particular genes to physical traits.

TRUE OR FALSE

T F

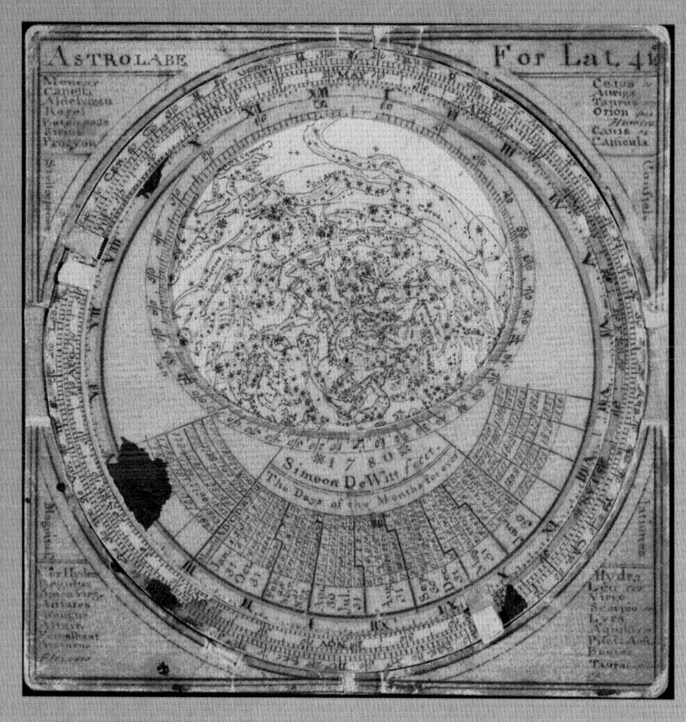

WHAT IS THIS MAP AND WHO CREATED IT?

SEQUOYAH
c. 1770–1843
Devised a method of writing for the Cherokee language

INVENTORS AND INNOVATORS

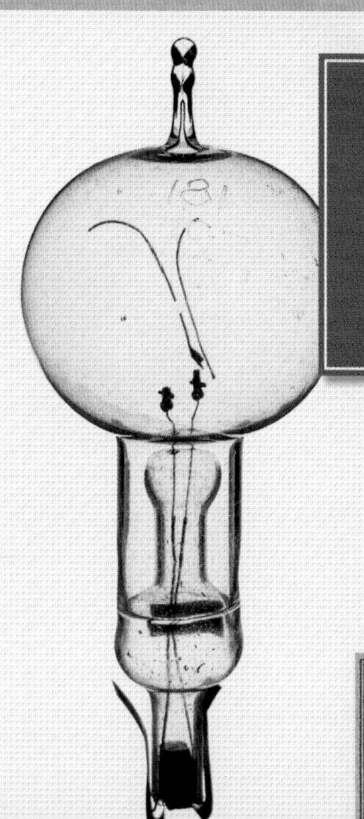

THOMAS EDISON
1847–1931
Inventions include: the gramophone, the incandescent light system, the megaphone, an energy storage battery, the electric valve, and the talking motion picture

JOHN STEVENS
1749–1838
Pioneer in steam-engine experimentation

NIKOLA TESLA

1856–1943

Introduced alternating-current electricity; lit the 1893 Chicago World's Columbian Exposition; harnessed and generated power from Niagara Falls

SOLOMON ANDREWS

1806–1872

Inventor of at least two dozen devices, including a gas lamp, a combination lock, and the world's first self-propelled, steerable airship

WHO PAINTED THIS PORTRAIT OF SAMUEL MORSE?

SAMUEL MORSE

1791–1872

Invented the telegraph

JONAS CHICKERING

1798–1853

Considered "the father of American piano making"

PATENT MODELS

Between the years 1790 and 1880 the U.S. Patent Office required both documentation and a three-dimensional working model to demonstrate each new invention submitted for a patent. These patent models provide a glimpse into the 19th century.

FIND THE MODEL

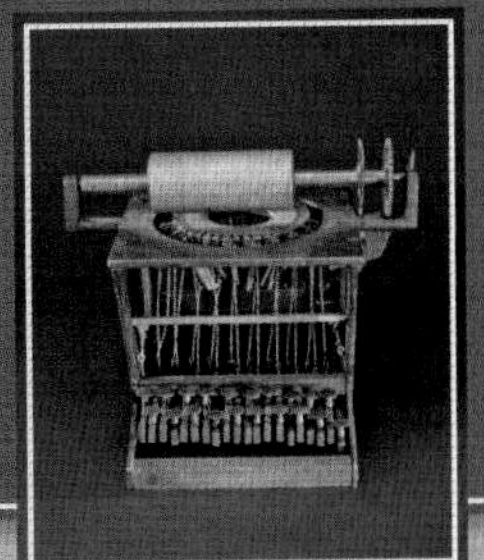

HEALTH AND WELLNESS

A number of people have contributed in different ways to the advancement of the medical field in the United States.

JOHNS HOPKINS

1795–1873

Hopkins, a nineteeth century Maryland merchant, banker, and investor, bequeathed $7 million to found a university, school of medicine, and hospital, and an affiliated training school for nurses. These institutions are credited with revolutionizing American medicine.

ELIZABETH BLACKWELL

1821–1910

Blackwell was the first woman to receive a medical degree, graduating at the head of her class from Geneva Medical College in 1849. Barred from practice in most hospitals, she opened her own clinic, which later became the New York Infirmary for Indigent Women and Children.

MARY WALKER

1832–1919

After becoming the second woman in the U.S. to earn a medical degree, Walker volunteered for the Union Army, serving near the front lines as a field surgeon for several years. In 1865, Walker was the first woman awarded the Congressional Medal of Honor.

CLARA BARTON

1821–1912

With the outbreak of the Civil War, Barton was shocked at the conditions and lack of medical relief supplies on the battlefields, and as superintendent of Union nurses, she worked tirelessly in the nursing of wounded soldiers at the front and in the distribution of much-needed supplies to the battlefield.

HARVEY CUSHING

1869–1939

A pioneer in his field, Cushing was considered the father of neurosurgery. Dr. Cushing was the first to use x-rays and to take blood pressure readings routinely during operations. He was also among the first to operate on the pituitary gland.

WILLIAM J. MAYO

1861–1939

CHARLES H. MAYO

1865–1939

The Mayo Brothers founded the Mayo Foundation for Medical Education and Research in affiliation with the University of Minnesota at Rochester.

LEARN MORE

CHARLES DREW

1904–1950

Charles Drew's most valuable contribution to medical science was his discovery and development of methods to preserve blood plasma. The application of his research and findings provided US Armed Forces with its first blood bank during World War II operations.

VIRGINIA APGAR

1909–1974

Apgar was a physician, anesthesiologist, and pioneer in research for the prevention and treatment of birth defects.

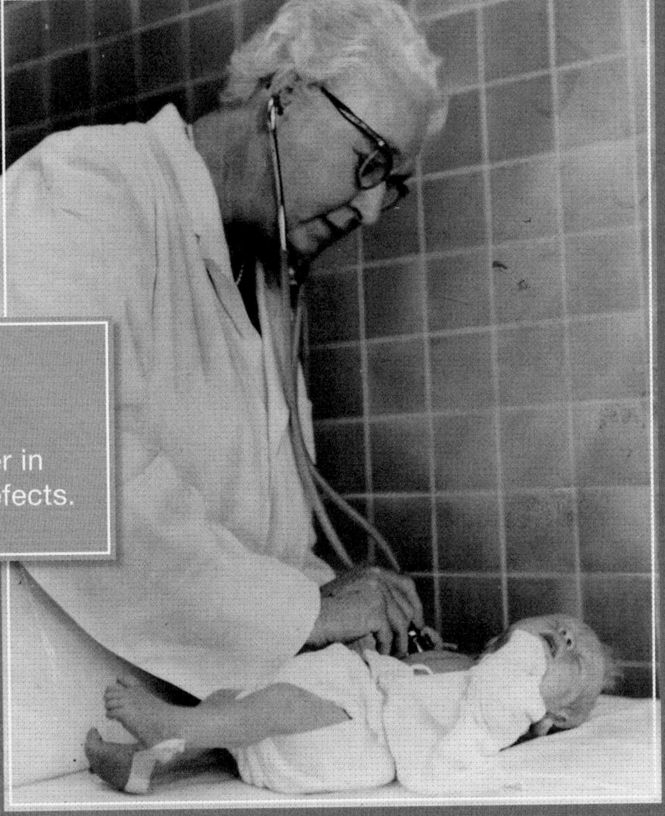

TRUE OR FALSE

T F

SPORTS HEROES

BASEBALL

JACKIE ROBINSON

1919–1972

- Broke the Major League Baseball color barrier in 1947
- Rookie of the Year in 1947
- Led the Brooklyn Dodgers to six pennants and one World Series title

A monument to Robinson, number 42, stands outside Dodger Stadium in Los Angeles.

GEORGE HERMAN "BABE" RUTH

1895–1948

- Led the Yankees to six American League Pennants and three World Series Championships
- In the 1927 season, hit sixty home runs, a record that stood for thirty-four years

LOU GEHRIG

1903–1941

- Played an incredible 2,130 consecutive games
- In thirteen consecutive seasons, drove in 100 or more runs

ROBERTO CLEMENTE

1934–1972

- Lifetime batting average of .317.
- Four National League batting championships
- National League MVP in 1966
- World Series MVP in 1971

KNUTE ROCKNE
1888–1931

- Head coach of the University of Notre Dame's football team between 1918 and 1930
- Led Notre Dame to six national championships and five undefeated seasons

VINCE LOMBARDI
1913–1970
As head coach of the Green Bay Packers, led them to two Super Bowl victories

JAMES NAISMITH
1861–1939
Invented basketball

WHICH BOXER?

JACK DEMPSEY

JOE LOUIS

SUGAR RAY ROBINSON

ROCKY MARCIANO

FRANCIS OUIMET
1893–1967

- Won the 1913 U.S. Open Golf Championship
- Ambassador for the sport

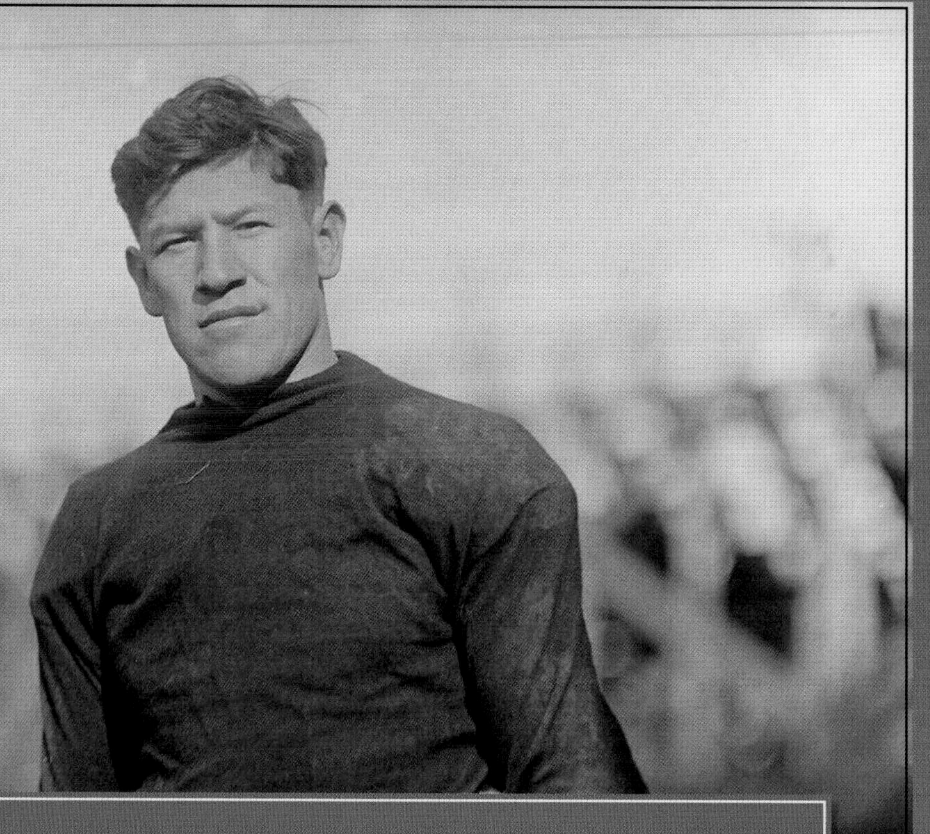

JIM THORPE

1888–1953

Native American Jim Thorpe was one of America's greatest athletes of the twentieth century. He came home a hero after winning gold medals in the traditional Pentathlon and Decathlon events at the 1912 Olympic Games in Stockholm, Sweden. Thorpe became the first athlete to win both the Pentathlon and Decathlon at a single modern Olympic Games.

REPRESENTING AMERICA: OLYMPIANS

HAZEL WIGHTMAN

1886–1974

At the 1924 Olympic Games in Paris, France, Wightman won gold in both doubles (with Helen Wills) and mixed doubles (with Richard Williams).

RAY EWRY

1873–1937

Ewry distinguished himself in three consecutive Olympic Games between 1900 and 1908. Ewry achieved the longest distance in the Standing Long Jump event and the highest height in the Standing High Jump event in each of these Olympic Games.

EDDIE EAGAN

1897–1967

Eddie Eagan is the only American to win a gold medal in a Summer and Winter Olympic Games.

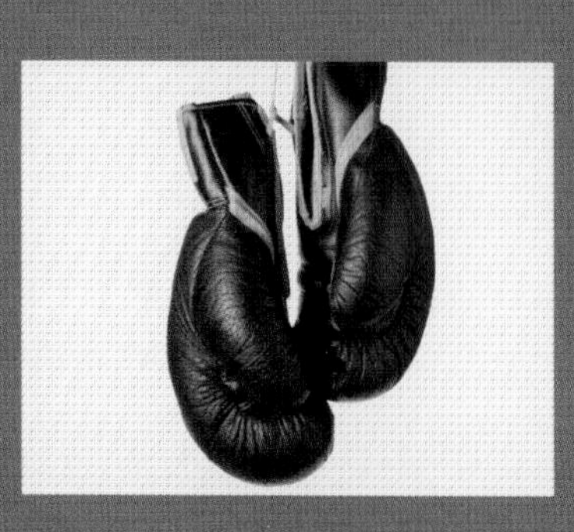

HELENE MADISON

1913–1970

In the 1932 Summer Olympic Games, competing in the Women's 100-meter freestyle, 400-meter freestyle and the 4 x 100-meter freestyle relay, Madison won gold medals and set Olympic or world records in each event.

DUKE KAHANAMOKU

1890–1968

Hawaiian folk hero, three-time Olympic gold medal swim champion and father of surfing, Kahanamoku won attention with his impressive performances in the 1912, 1920 and 1932 Olympics.

WHAT WAS THE "MIRACLE ON ICE" AND WHEN DID IT TAKE PLACE?

BABE ZAHARIAS

1911–1956

In the 1932 Summer Olympic Games held in Los Angeles, California, Mildred "Babe" Didrikson Zaharias, a Renaissance Sportswoman, competed in the Women's Javelin Throw, 80-meter Hurdles and the High Jump.

WILMA RUDOLPH

1940–1994

Rudolph won a bronze medal in the 1956 Olympic Games in Melbourne, Australia. She then went on to shine in the 1960 Summer Olympic Games in Rome, Italy. After winning three gold medals in sprint events (the 100-meter, 200-meter, and 4-x-100-meter relay events), Rudolph was dubbed "the world's fastest woman."

HOW MANY MEDALS?

3 5
10 22

JESSE OWENS

1913–1980

At the 1936 Olympic Games in Berlin, Jesse Owens stunned the world by capturing four gold medals in track and field (100-meter, 200-meter, long jump and 4x100-meter relay events).

PHINEAS BARNUM

1810–1891

By the time he created "the greatest show on earth" in 1872, he enjoyed an international reputation as a showman who could be counted on to amaze and delight audiences with performers and attractions of every description—all served up with a generous dose of the "humbug" that was Barnum's specialty.

LARGER THAN LIFE

Some of the people on this page were real, others fictional. All have contributed to American myths and folk tales, reflecting certain aspects of the American experience.

DAVY CROCKETT

1786–1836

Unlike his solitary predecessor Daniel Boone, Davy Crockett created the image of the frontiersman as a jocular, colorful "type" who loved tall tales, whisky, and cutting a caper. After serving in Congress, Crockett created a road show in which he presented himself to civilized eastern audiences as the wild and woolly backwoodsman, "half man, half alligator." Still restless, however, Crockett joined the fight for Texas independence and was killed at the Alamo.

WILLIAM "BUFFALO BILL" CODY

1846–1917

Cody, originally a frontier scout, Indian fighter, and buffalo hunter, had become famous as the hero of "Buffalo Bill" dime novels and magazine stories. In 1882 he created his popular wild west show and toured as its star for thirty years, arguably doing more than any single American to popularize the myth of the West.

DID YOU KNOW ROSIE THE RIVETER HAS HER OWN SONG?

WAS THERE A REAL UNCLE SAM?

FAMOUS FOLK HEROES

GAME

MIGHTY CASEY

PAUL BUNYAN

PECOS BILL

JOHN HENRY

WHAT DO YOU KNOW?

WHO WAS A QUAKER ABOLITIONIST?

Benjamin Banneker | Benjamin Lay

WHO WAS A FAMOUS ACTRESS?

Charlotte Cushman | Charlotte Perkins Gilman

WHO WAS AN EDUCATION REFORMER?

Horace Mann | Horace Greeley

WHO WAS A PHOTOGRAPHER?

Dorothea Dix | Dorothea Lange

WHO WAS A NAVAL HERO?

John Paul Jones | John Russwurm

WHO WAS AN ANTHROPOLOGIST?

Zora Neale Hurston | Barbara McClintock

WHO HEADED THE U.S. EXPLORING EXPEDITION?

Charles Wilkes | John Wesley Powell

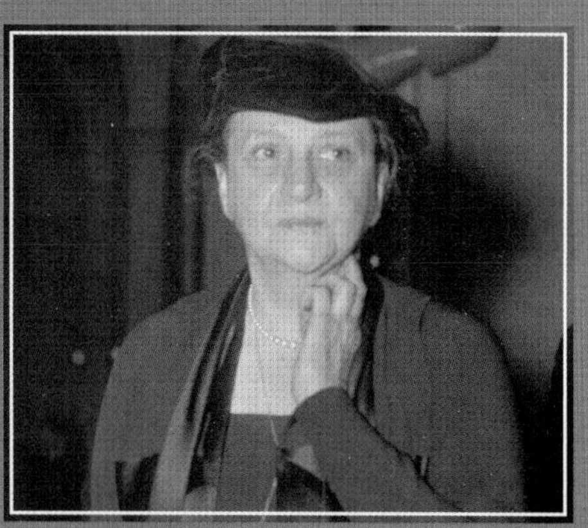

WHO WAS A RUNNER?

Wilma Rudolph | Duke Kahanamoku

WHO WAS FRANKLIN ROOSEVELT'S SECRETARY OF LABOR?

Fannie Lou Hamer | Frances Perkins